PREFACE

Welcome to "Donate Wisely to Charity Organizations : A Guide for Individual Donors"! As a donor, you have the power to make a meaningful difference in the world. With so many charities and causes vying for your attention and support, it's essential to approach your philanthropy with intention and strategy.

The Importance of Informed Giving

Informed giving is crucial to ensuring that your donations are used effectively and efficiently. By understanding the charities you support, evaluating their financial health and governance, you can maximize your philanthropic efforts and create lasting change.

A Guide for Individual Donors

This handbook is designed specifically for individual donors like you. Whether you're a seasoned philanthropist or just starting out, "Donate Wisely" will provide you with the knowledge, tools, and guidance you need to make informed decisions.

Our Goal

Our goal is to empower you to become a wise and effective donor, capable of making informed decisions about your charitable giving. By providing you with practical advice, real-world examples, and expert insights, we hope to help you achieve your philanthropic goals and make a meaningful difference in the wor

DONATE WISELY TO CHARITY ORGANIZATIONS
A GUIDE FOR INDIVIDUAL DONORS
TABLE OF CONTENTS

CHAPTER 1: CHARITY ORGANIZATIONS: AN OVERVIEW OF NOTABLE ORGANIZATIONS

Introduction

With thousands of charity organizations working towards various causes, it can be overwhelming to choose which ones to support. In this chapter, we'll provide an in-depth look at notable charity organizations, highlighting their mission, focus areas, impact, and what makes them effective.

International Organizations

1. UNICEF : The United Nations Children's Fund

- Mission: Improve the lives of children and mothers around the world
- Focus areas: Health, education, protection, and emergency response
- Impact: Vaccination programs, education initiatives, and advocacy for children's rights

2. UNESCO : The United Nations Educational, Scientific and Cultural Organization

- Mission: Promote peace and security through international cooperation in education, science, culture, and communication
- Focus areas: Education, science, culture, and communication
- Impact: Promoting cultural diversity, protecting heritage sites, and advancing

3. Red Cross : The International Red Cross and Red Crescent Movement .

 Mission: Provide humanitarian aid and support to individuals affected by disasters, conflicts, and health crises .
 Focus areas: Disaster response, health services, and promoting humanitarian values .
 Impact: Providing emergency assistance, promoting disaster preparedness, and advocating for humanitarian law .

Health Organizations .
1. St. Jude Children's Research Hospital .
 Mission: Find cures for children with cancer and other life-threatening diseases .
 Focus areas: Pediatric cancer research, treatment, and care .
 Impact: Advancing cancer research, providing free medical care, and supporting families .

2. Doctors Without Borders/ Médecins Sans Frontières (MSF) .

 Mission: Provide medical care to people affected by conflict, epidemics, disasters, or exclusion from healthcare .
 Focus areas: Emergency medical care, and advocacy for access to healthcare .

 Impact: Providing medical care in crisis situations, responding to epidemics, and promoting access to healthcare .

Educational Organizations

1. Don Bosco

 Mission: Provide education and vocational training to disadvantaged youth .

 Focus areas: Education, vocational training, and youth development .

 Impact: Empowering youth, promoting education, and supporting community development .

2. Pratham

 Mission: Improve the quality of education for underprivileged children .

 Focus areas: Education, research, and advocacy.

 Impact: Improving learning outcomes, promoting education for all, and advocating for education policy reform .

Child Welfare Organizations

1. CRY (Child Rights and You)

 Mission: Protect and promote the rights of children

 Focus areas: Education, health, protection, and advocacy

 Impact: Supporting children's education, health, and protection.

2. Save the Children

 Mission: Promote children's rights and provide support to children in need

 Focus areas: Education, health, protection, and emergency response

 Impact: Providing emergency assistance, promoting education, and advocating for children's rights

Environmental Organizations

1. The Nature Conservancy

 Mission: Protect ecosystems and preserve natural habitats

 Focus areas: Conservation, research, and advocacy

 Impact: Protecting biodiversity, and promoting sustainable practices

2. WWF (World Wildlife Fund)

 Mission: Conserve nature and reduce the most pressing threats to the diversity of life on Earth. .

 Focus areas: Conservation, research, and advocacy
.

 Impact: Protecting endangered species, promoting sustainable practices, and conserving natural habitats
.

Corporate-Funded Foundations   .

1. Bill and Melinda Gates Foundation   .

 Mission: Improve global health, education, and poverty alleviation
.

 Focus areas: Global health, education, poverty alleviation, and access to technology   .

 Impact: The foundation has made significant contributions to global health, including: .

 Vaccination efforts: Supported vaccination programs that have helped prevent millions of deaths from diseases like polio, measles, and rotavirus.
.

 Disease eradication: Contributed to efforts to eradicate diseases like polio and malaria.   .

 Education: Supported initiatives to improve access to quality education, particularly in underserved communities.   .

2. Ford Foundation

- Mission: Reduce inequality and promote social justice
- Focus areas: Economic opportunity, education, and human rights
- Impact: The foundation has:
- Supported economic empowerment programs: Provided funding for initiatives that promote economic opportunity and stability for marginalized communities.
- Advanced human rights: Worked to promote human rights and social justice, particularly for vulnerable populations.
- Improved education: Supported initiatives to improve access to quality education and promote educational equity.

3. Wellcome Trust

- Mission: Improve global health through medical research and innovation
- Focus areas: Medical research, global health, and innovation
- Impact: The trust has:

□ Advanced medical research: Supported groundbreaking research in areas like infectious diseases, mental health, and climate change.

□ Improved global health: Contributed to efforts to address pressing global health challenges, including outbreaks and epidemics.

4. Amnesty International

□ Mission: Amnesty International is a global movement that campaigns for human rights and promotes justice, freedom, and dignity for all people. Their mission is to protect and promote human rights, and to advocate for those whose rights are being violated. .

□ Focus Area: Amnesty International focuses on a wide range of human rights issues, including: .

□ Freedom of expression and assembly : Protecting people's right to express themselves and assemble peacefully. .

□ Torture and ill-treatment : Campaigning against torture and ill-treatment, and promoting humane treatment of all individuals. .

□ Death penalty : Working to abolish the death penalty worldwide. .

□ Refugees and migrants : Advocating for the rights of refugees and migrants, and promoting humane treatment and protection. .

□ Women's rights : Promoting women's rights and combating violence against women. .

□ Impact: Amnesty International has had a significant impact on human rights globally, including: .

AMNESTY INTERNATIONAL

☐ Influencing policy and law : Amnesty International's research and advocacy have influenced policy and law changes in many countries, protecting human rights and promoting justice.

☐ Mobilizing public opinion : Amnesty International's campaigns have mobilized millions of people worldwide, raising awareness about human rights issues and promoting action.

☐ Protecting human rights defenders : Amnesty International has provided support and protection to human rights defenders, activists, and journalists who are at risk.   .

☐ Promoting accountability : Amnesty International has promoted accountability for human rights abuses, advocating for those responsible to be brought   to   justice.   .

Evaluating Charity Organizations

When considering supporting a charity organization, it's essential to evaluate their:

1. Mission and goals : Ensure alignment with your values and philanthropic objectives.

2. Financial transparency : Review their financial statements and governance practices.

3. Impact and effectiveness : Evaluate their programs, outcomes, and impact.
4. Accountability and governance : Assess their leadership, governance structure, and accountability mechanisms.   .

Conclusion

By understanding the mission, focus areas, and impact of these notable charity organizations, you can make informed decisions about which organizations to support and how to maximize your philanthropic impact.   .

CHAPTER 2: THE POWER OF DONATING: WHY YOUR CONTRIBUTIONS MATTER

Introduction

As you consider donating to a charity or cause, you're taking the first step towards making a positive impact in the world. In this chapter, we'll explore the significance of individual donations and how they can collectively drive meaningful change.

The Impact of Individual Donations

1. Changing Lives :

Individual donations can have a profound impact on people's lives. Whether it's providing medical care, education, or basic necessities, your contribution can make a tangible difference.

a) Example : Donations to organizations that provide disaster relief can help individuals and communities recover from natural disasters.

b) Example : Contributions to education-focused organizations can help improve access to quality education for underprivileged students.

2. Driving Social Change :

Donating can also drive social change by supporting causes that promote equality, justice, and human rights.

a) Example : Donations to organizations that advocate for human rights can help promote social justice and equality.

b) Example : Contributions to environmental organizations can help support initiatives that promote sustainability and conservation.

3. Supporting Causes :

By donating to a specific cause, you're helping to drive progress and raise awareness about important issues. Your support can also inspire others to get involved.

4. Empowering Communities :

Donations can empower communities by providing resources, infrastructure, and opportunities for growth. This, in turn, can lead to sustainable development and long-term positive change.

a) Example : Donations to community development organizations can help support initiatives that promote economic growth, education, and community engagement.

5. Influencing Policy :

Collective donations can influence policy decisions and shape the direction of social and environmental initiatives. By supporting organizations working towards a common goal, you're contributing to a larger movement.

The Benefits of Donating

Donating not only benefits the recipients but also has benefits for the donor. Some of the benefits of donating include:

1. Personal Fulfillment :

Donating can give you a sense of purpose and fulfillment, knowing that your contributions are making a positive impact.

2. Tax Benefits :

Donating to qualified charitable organizations can provide tax benefits, such as deductions and credits.

3. Networking Opportunities :

Donating can provide opportunities to network with like-minded individuals and organizations, potentially leading to new relationships and collaborations.

The Power of Collective Giving

1. Amplifying Impact :

When individuals donate, they set an example for others. This can inspire a chain reaction of kindness and generosity, ultimately leading to a more compassionate society.

2. Creating a Sense of Community :

Donating can foster a sense of community among like-minded individuals. By working together towards a common goal, donors can build connections and share experiences.

3. Inspiring Others :

When individuals come together to donate, their collective efforts can lead to significant positive change. This amplifies the impact of individual donations and creates a ripple effect.

Why Your Contributions Matter

1. Every Amount Counts : Regardless of the amount, every donation matters. Even small contributions can add up and make a significant difference when combined with others.
2. Personal Fulfillment : Donating can bring a sense of personal fulfillment and purpose.
3. Legacy : Your donations can leave a lasting legacy, contributing to long-term positive change and inspiring future generations.   .
4. Collective Impact : When combined with the contributions of others, your donation can have a significant collective impact.   .
5. Setting an Example : Your contributions can set an example for others, inspiring them to give and make a difference.   .

Conclusion

Individual donations have the power to drive meaningful change and create a lasting impact. By understanding the significance of your contributions, you'll be empowered to make informed decisions and maximize your giving. .

CHAPTER 3: DEFINING YOUR GIVING GOALS: WHAT DRIVES YOUR HILANTHROPY?

Introduction

Before donating to a charity or cause, it's essential to define your giving goals and understand what drives your philanthropy. By clarifying your values and objectives, you'll be able to make informed decisions and ensure your donations align with your passions and priorities.

Understanding Your Personal Values

1. Reflecting on Your Values :

Take time to reflect on what matters most to you. Consider your personal experiences, beliefs, and priorities. What issues do you feel strongly about? What kind of impact do you want to make ?

2. Identifying Your Core Values :

Write down your core values, such as:
- Education
- Healthcare
- Environmental conservation
- Social justice
- Animal welfare
- Community development

3. Prioritizing Your Values :

Rank your values in order of importance. This will help you focus on the causes that matter most to you.

Defining Your Giving Objectives

1. What Do You Want to Achieve? : Consider what you want to achieve through your donations. Do you want to :

 Support a specific cause or issue?   .
 Make a tangible impact in a particular community or region?   .
 Contribute to long-term systemic change? .
 Honor a loved one or memorialize an event?

2. Setting Specific Goals :

Write down specific, measurable, achievable, relevant, and time-bound (SMART) goals for your giving. For example: .

 "I want to support education initiatives in underprivileged communities, with a focus on literacy programs for children."   .

 "I aim to donate $X annually to environmental conservation efforts, with a focus on wildlife preservation."   .

Considering Your Giving Style

1. Reactive vs. Proactive Giving :

Consider whether you prefer reactive giving or proactive giving .   .

2. Hands-on vs. Hands-off Giving :

Think about whether you want to be directly involved in the charitable work or prefer to support organizations that handle the implementation.

Creating a Personal Giving Framework
1. Giving Mission Statement :
Write a personal giving mission statement that outlines your values, objectives, and goals. This will serve as a guide for your philanthropic efforts.

2. Giving Budget :

Determine how much you can realistically donate each year, considering your financial situation and other commitments.

3. Giving Timeline :

Consider whether you want to donate regularly (eg, monthly, annually) or make one-time donations.

Conclusion

Defining your giving goals and understanding your personal values and objectives is crucial to effective philanthropy. By creating a personal framework for giving, you'll be able to make informed decisions and ensure your donations align with your passions and priorities. In the next chapter, we'll explore how to research and evaluate charities to ensure your donations are used effectively.

CHAPTER 4: FINDING THE RIGHT CHARITY: RESEARCH TOOLS AND RESOURCES

Introduction

With countless charities and causes to choose from, finding the right one can be overwhelming.

Charity Evaluators

1. Overview of Charity Evaluators :

Charity evaluators assess non-profits based on financial stability, governance, and impact. Examples include:

☐ Charity Navigator (charitynavigator.org)

☐ GuideStar (guidestar.org)

☐ BBB Wise Giving Alliance (give.org)

☐ GreatNonprofits (greatnonprofits.org)

2. How Evaluators Assess Charities :

Understand the criteria used by evaluators, such as:

☐ Financial health (eg, overhead ratio, revenue growth)

☐ Governance and transparency (eg, board composition, reporting practices)

☐ Program effectiveness (eg, outcomes, impact)

Ratings and Reviews

1. Understanding Ratings Systems :

Familiarize yourself with rating systems, such as:

☐ Charity Navigator's star ratings (0-4 stars)

2. Reading Reviews and Feedback :

Explore reviews from donors, and beneficiaries to gain insights into a charity's work.

Additional Research Resources

1. Non-Profit Databases :

Utilize databases like:

☐ Foundation Directory Online (foundationcenter.org)

☐ Nonprofit Leadership Alliance's database (nonprofitleadershipalliance.org)

2. Government Databases :

Leverage government databases, such as:

☐ IRS Form 990 database (irs.gov)

☐ State charity registration databases

3. Social Media and Online Research :

Research charities on social media platforms to gauge their reputation, and transparency.

Tips for Effective Research

1. Verify Charity Information :

Verify a charity's information, including their mission, programs, and financials.

2. Evaluate Multiple Sources :

Consult multiple evaluators and resources to get a comprehensive view of a charity.

3. Understand Limitations :

Recognize the limitations of ratings and reviews, and consider additional factors, such as:

☐ Program-specific effectiveness

☐ Leadership and governance
☐ Financial sustainability

Tips for Researching Charities

Here are some tips for researching charities: .
1. Verify a charity's legitimacy : Check if a charity is registered with the relevant authorities.   .
2. Read reviews and ratings : Check online reviews and ratings from other donors.   .
3. Evaluate a charity's website : Review a charity's website to understand their mission, programs, and   finances.   .
4. Contact the charity directly : Reach out to a charity   directly.   .

Common Red Flags

When researching charities, be aware of the following   red   flags: .
1. Lack of transparency : A charity that is not transparent about their finances, governance, or programs.   .
2. Poor governance : A charity with ineffective board   of   directors.   .
3. Ineffective programs : A charity with programs that   are   not   effective.   .
4. High administrative costs : A charity with high administrative   costs.   .

Conclusion

Finding the right charity requires thorough research and evaluation. By utilizing charity evaluators, ratings, and reviews, you'll be equipped to make informed decisions that align with your values and goals.   .

CHAPTER 5: EVALUATING CHARITY EFFECTIVENESS: FINANCIALS, GOVERNANCE, AND IMPACT

Introduction

When evaluating a charity's effectiveness, it's essential to consider key metrics and accountability measures. In this chapter, we'll explore financials, governance, and impact, providing you with a comprehensive framework for assessment.

Financial Evaluation

1. Financial Statements :

Review a charity's financial statements, including:
 Statement of Financial Position (Balance Sheet)
 Statement of Activities (Income Statement)
 Statement of Cash Flows

2. Key Financial Metrics :

 Program Expense Ratio : Percentage of expenses dedicated to programs (target: 80% or higher)
 Administrative Expense Ratio : Percentage of expenses dedicated to administration (target: 15% or lower)

 Fundraising Expense Ratio : Percentage of expenses dedicated to fundraising (target: 5% or lower) .

 Revenue Growth : Consistency and sustainability of revenue streams .

3. Financial Health :

Assess a charity's financial stability, including: .

 Reserve Funds : Availability of funds for unexpected expenses or opportunities .

 Debt Ratio : Level of indebtedness and financial leverage .

Governance Evaluation

1. Board of Directors :

Assess the board's: .

 Independence : Mix of internal and external board members .

 Expertise : Relevant skills and experience among board members .

 Involvement : Level of engagement and oversight .

2. Governance Practices :

Evaluate a charity's: .

 Transparency : Availability of governance documents and financial information .

 Conflict of Interest Policy : Procedures for managing conflicts of interest .

 Whistleblower Policy : Protections for reporting wrongdoing or concerns .

Impact Evaluation

1. Program Outcomes :

Assess a charity's: .

 Effectiveness : Achievement of program goals and objectives .

 Efficiency : Resource utilization and cost-effectiveness.   .

2. Impact Measurement :
Evaluate a charity's: .
 Metrics and Indicators : Use of relevant metrics to track progress.   .
 Evaluation Methods : Approaches to assessing program effectiveness   .

 3. Reporting and Transparency :
Assess a charity's: .
 Annual Reports : Availability and content of annual reports   .
 Progress Updates : Regular updates on program progress and impact.   .

Accountability Measures

1. Accreditation and Certification :
Look for accreditations and certifications, such as: .
 Better Business Bureau's Wise Giving Alliance accreditation   .
 Charity Navigator's Seal of Transparency.

2. Independent Audits :
Evaluate a charity's: .
 Audit Committee : Presence and role of an audit committee   .
 Audit Report : Availability and content of independent audit reports   .

3. Transparency and Disclosure :
Assess a charity's: .
 Website Transparency : Availability of information on the charity's website   .
 Disclosure Practices : Willingness to provide information upon request   .

Key Performance Indicators (KPIs)

When evaluating a charity's effectiveness, consider the following KPIs:

1. Program expense ratio :

The percentage of expenses spent on programs.

2. Administrative expense ratio :

The percentage of expenses spent on administration.

3. Fundraising expense ratio :

The percentage of expenses spent on fundraising.

4. Donor retention rate :

The percentage of donors retained from year to year.

Red Flags

When evaluating a charity's effectiveness, be aware of the following red flags:

1. Low program expense ratio :

A charity with a low program expense ratio may be inefficient or ineffective.

2. High administrative costs :
A charity with high administrative costs may be inefficient or bureaucratic.

3. Lack of transparency :
A charity that lacks transparency may be hiding something.

4. Poor governance :
A charity with poor governance may be at risk of mismanagement or corruption.

Best Practices
When evaluating charity effectiveness, consider the following best practices:

1. Use multiple evaluation criteria :
Use a range of evaluation criteria to get a comprehensive picture of a charity's effectiveness.

2. Review financial statements :
Review a charity's financial statements to understand their financial position and stability.

3. Evaluate governance and leadership :
Evaluate a charity's governance and leadership to ensure they are effective and accountable.

4. Assess impact and outcomes :
Assess a charity's impact and outcomes to ensure they are effective and efficient.

Conclusion
Evaluating a charity's effectiveness requires a comprehensive assessment of financials, governance, and impact. By understanding key metrics and accountability measures, you'll be equipped to make informed decisions and support charities that demonstrate strong performance and transparency.

CHAPTER 6: DONATION OPTIONS: ONE-TIME, RECURRING, AND PLANNED GIVING

Introduction

Lorem ipsum dolor sit amet, consectetur adipiscing elit, sed do eiusmod tempor

One-Time Donations

1. Definition :

A one-time donation is a single gift made to a charity, usually in response to a specific need or campaign.   .

2. Benefits :

 Flexibility :

One-time donations allow you to respond to immediate needs or opportunities.   .

 Simplicity :

Easy to make, with minimal commitment.   .

3. Examples :

 Responding to disaster relief efforts   .
 Supporting a specific project or initiative .
 making a memorial donation   .

Recurring Donations
1. Definition :
A recurring donation is a regular, ongoing gift made to a charity, typically monthly or annually.
2. Benefits :

☐ Sustainability : Provides charities with predictable income and allows for long-term planning.   .

☐ Impact : Enables charities to make a more significant impact over time.   .
3. Examples :

☐ Monthly giving programs   .

☐ Sponsorship programs for children or animals   .
Planned Giving
1. Definition :
Planned giving involves making a charitable gift through a will, trust, or other financial vehicle, often with tax benefits.   .
2. Benefits :
☐ Legacy : Allows you to leave a lasting legacy and support your favorite causes beyond your lifetime.   .

☐ Tax Benefits : May provide tax deductions or other benefits.   .
3. Examples :
☐ bequests in a will
☐ Charitable trusts or foundations
☐ Donor-advised funds
Other Donation Options
1. In-Kind Donations : Donating goods or services instead of cash.

2. Volunteer Time : Donating time and skills to support a charity's work.

3. Matching Gifts :

Employer-matched donations, where your employer matches your gift to a charity.   .

Considerations

1. Personal Financial Situation :

Consider your financial situation and goals when deciding on a donation type.   .

2. Charity's Needs :

Consider the charity's needs and goals when choosing a donation type.   .

3. Tax Implications :

Lorem ipsum dolor sit amet, consectetur adipiscing elit, sed do eiusmod tempor

Choosing the Right Donation Option :

When choosing a donation option, consider the following factors: .

1. Financial situation :

Consider your financial situation and ability to make donations.   .

2. Philanthropic goals :

Consider your philanthropic goals and the impact you want to make.   .

3. Personal preferences :

Consider your personal preferences and values.   .

Conclusion

Understanding the different donation options available can help you make informed decisions and maximize your impact. Whether you choose to make a one-time donation, recurring donation, or planned gift, your support can make a significant difference in the lives of others. In the next chapter, we'll explore strategies for maximizing your impact and creating lasting change.

CHAPTER 7: STRATEGIC GIVING: MAXIMIZING YOUR IMPACT

Introduction

Strategic giving involves thoughtful and intentional philanthropy, aimed at maximizing impact and creating lasting change. In this chapter, we'll explore tips and strategies for optimizing your donations and achieving your philanthropic goals.

Understanding Your Goals

1. Define Your Objectives :

Clearly define what you want to achieve through your philanthropy, such as:

- Supporting a specific cause or issue
- creating systemic change
- Empowering marginalized communities

2. Research and Due Diligence :

Research potential recipient organizations and evaluate their:

- Mission alignment : Ensure alignment with your goals and values
- Effectiveness : Assess their track record and impact
- Transparency and accountability : Evaluate their governance, financials, and reporting practices

Key Principles of Strategic Giving:
Strategic giving involves several key principles, including:
1. Clear goals :
Establishing clear goals and objectives for your philanthropy.
2. Research and due diligence :
Conducting thorough research on potential recipient organizations.
3. Strategic planning :
Developing a strategic plan for your philanthropy, including a budget and timeline.
4. Collaboration and partnership :
Collaborating with other donors, and stakeholders to amplify your impact.
5. Evaluation and assessment :
Regularly evaluating and assessing the impact of your philanthropy.
Maximizing Your Impact :
To maximize your impact, consider the following strategies:
1. Focus on root causes :
Addressing the underlying causes of social problems.
2. Support effective organizations :
Supporting organizations that are effective, efficient, and transparent.
3. Invest in sustainable solutions :
Investing in solutions that are sustainable and have long-term impact.
4. Engage in advocacy :
Engaging in advocacy and policy change efforts to address systemic issues.

Effective Philanthropy:
Effective philanthropy involves several key elements, including:

1. Clear theory of change :
Having a clear theory of change and understanding how your philanthropy will make a difference.

2. Strong relationships :
Building strong relationships with the organizations and people you support.

3. Flexibility and adaptability :
Being flexible and adaptable in your philanthropic approach.

4. Continuous learning :
Continuously learning and improving your philanthropic approach.

Strategic Giving Strategies

1. Focus on Root Causes :
Address underlying issues rather than just symptoms, such as:

☐ Supporting education initiatives to address poverty

☐ Funding research to address disease prevention

2. Support Innovative Solutions :
Encourage innovative approaches and solutions, such as:

☐ Funding pilot programs or research initiatives.

☐ Supporting social entrepreneurship

3. Collaborate and Partner :
Partner with other donors, organizations, or stakeholders to:

☐ Amplify impact : Increase the scale and reach of your philanthropy

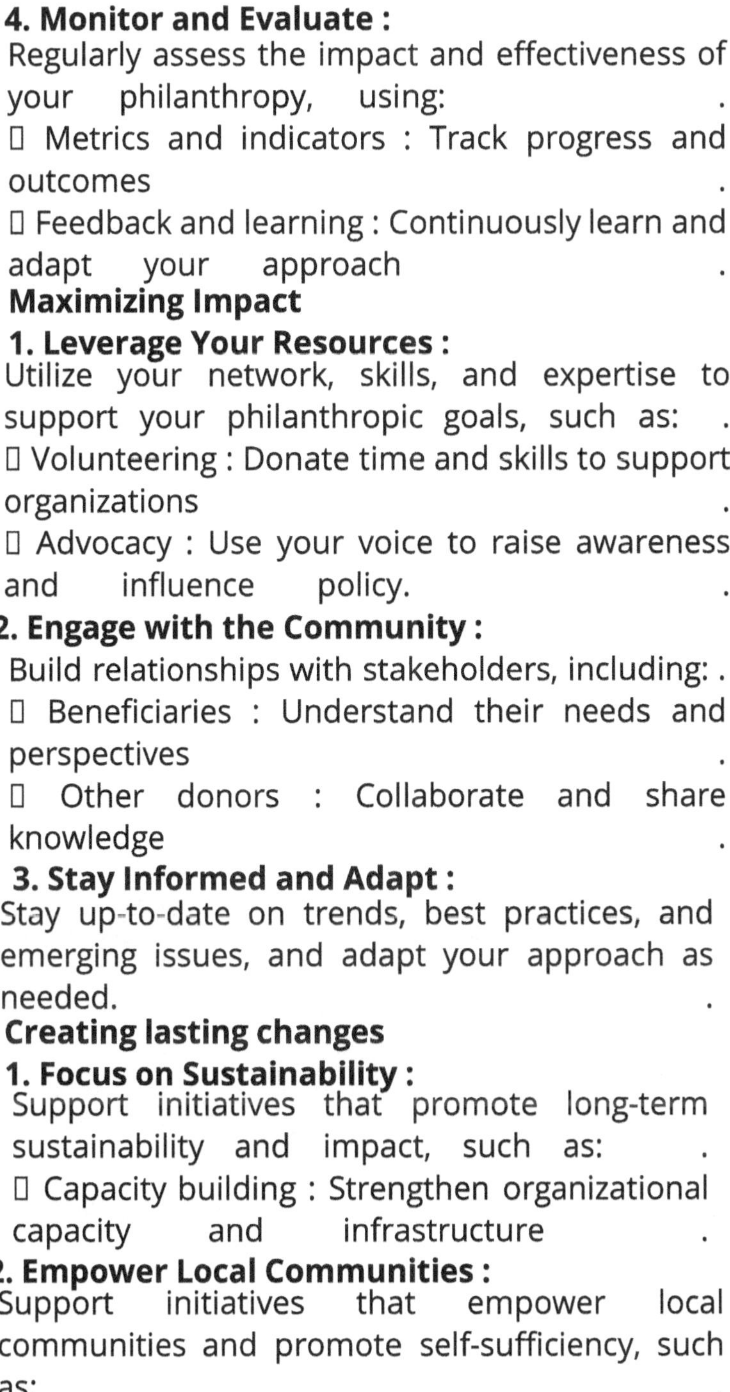

4. Monitor and Evaluate :
Regularly assess the impact and effectiveness of your philanthropy, using:
- Metrics and indicators : Track progress and outcomes
- Feedback and learning : Continuously learn and adapt your approach

Maximizing Impact

1. Leverage Your Resources :
Utilize your network, skills, and expertise to support your philanthropic goals, such as:
- Volunteering : Donate time and skills to support organizations
- Advocacy : Use your voice to raise awareness and influence policy.

2. Engage with the Community :
Build relationships with stakeholders, including:
- Beneficiaries : Understand their needs and perspectives
- Other donors : Collaborate and share knowledge

3. Stay Informed and Adapt :
Stay up-to-date on trends, best practices, and emerging issues, and adapt your approach as needed.

Creating lasting changes

1. Focus on Sustainability :
Support initiatives that promote long-term sustainability and impact, such as:
- Capacity building : Strengthen organizational capacity and infrastructure

2. Empower Local Communities :
Support initiatives that empower local communities and promote self-sufficiency, such as:

 Community-led initiatives : Support initiatives led by local communities .
 Capacity building : Strengthen local capacity and infrastructure .

3. Evaluate Legacy :

Consider the lasting impact of your philanthropy and how it will continue to benefit future generations. .

Conclusion

Strategic giving requires thoughtful and intentional philanthropy, aimed at maximizing impact and creating lasting change. By understanding your goals, researching potential recipient organizations, and utilizing strategic giving strategies, you can optimize your donations and achieve your philanthropic goals. In the next chapter, we'll explore how to build relationships with charities and stay engaged.

CHAPTER 8: BUILDING RELATIONSHIPS: COMMUNICATING WITH CHARITIES

Introduction

Building relationships with charities is essential for effective philanthropy. By communicating with charities, you can gain a deeper understanding of their work, build trust, and make informed decisions about your donations.

Contacting Charities

1. Finding the Right Contact :

Identify the right person or department to contact, such as:

- Donor relations : For questions about donations and giving opportunities
- Program staff : For questions about specific programs or initiatives

2. Initial Contact :

Reach out to the charity via:

- Phone : Call the charity's main number or donor relations department
- Email : Send an email to the charity's general inbox or donor relations department

Building Relationships and Community

 Website contact form : Use the charity's website contact form to send a message.   .

3. Preparing Questions :

Prepare thoughtful questions to ask the charity, such as: .

 Mission and goals : What is the charity's mission, and what are its goals?   .

 Impact and outcomes : What impact has the charity made, and what outcomes has it achieved?   .

Understanding Charity Work

1. Reviewing Annual Reports :

Review the charity's annual report to gain insights into: .

 Financial performance : The charity's financial health and sustainability   .

 Program impact : The impact and effectiveness of the charity's programs.   .

 Governance and leadership : The charity's governance structure and leadership team   .

2. Exploring Website and Social Media :

Explore the charity's website and social media channels to: .

 Stay up-to-date : Learn about the charity's latest news, updates, and initiatives   .

 Engage with the charity : Interact with the charity on social media and share their content

3. Attending Events and Meetings :

Attend charity events and meetings to:

 Meet staff and leadership : Build relationships with charity staff and leadership

 Learn about programs : Gain a deeper understanding of the charity's programs and initiatives

Why Build Relationships with Charities ?

Building relationships with charities can have numerous benefits, including: .

1. Increased trust :
Building trust with charities can help you feel more confident in their ability to use your donations effectively.   .

 2. Better understanding :
Understanding a charity's goals, needs, and challenges can help you make more informed decisions about your donations.   .

3. Improved communication :
Effective communication can help prevent misunderstandings and ensure that your donations are used as intended.   .

Communicating with Charities:
Effective communication is key to building strong relationships with charities. Consider the following tips: .

1. Be clear and concise :
Clearly communicate your goals, expectations, and concerns.   .

2. Be respectful :
Treat charity staff and volunteers with respect and professionalism.   .

3. Be open-minded :
Be open to new ideas and perspectives.   .

4. Be responsive :

Respond promptly to charity communications and requests.   .

Types of Communication:
There are several types of communication that can help you build relationships with charities, including:

1. Email :
Email can be a convenient way to communicate with charities, especially for routine updates and questions.   .

2. Phone :

Phone calls can be a good way to have more in-depth conversations with charity staff.   .

3. In-person meetings :
In-person meetings can provide an opportunity to build more personal relationships and discuss complex issues.   .

4. Social media :
Social media can be a good way to stay up -to -date on charity news and events. .

Best Practices for Communicating with Charities: .

Consider the following best practices for communicating with charities: .

1. Set clear expectations :
Clearly communicate your expectations and goals.   .

2. Ask questions :
Don't be afraid to ask questions if you're unsure about something.   .

3. Provide feedback :
Provide feedback to charities on their programs and services.   .

4. Show appreciation :
Express gratitude for the charity's work and the impact of your donations.   .

Building Relationships

1. Establishing Trust :
Build trust with the charity by: .

 Being transparent : Being open and transparent about your giving goals and expectations .

2. Providing Feedback :
Provide feedback to the charity on: .
 Programs and services : Share your thoughts and suggestions on the charity's programs and services . .
 Communication and reporting : .Provide feedback on the charity's communication and reporting practices. .

3. Staying Engaged :
Stay engaged with the charity by: .
 Volunteering : Donating time and skills to support the charity's work. .
 Advocating : Sharing the charity's work with others and advocating for their cause. .

Conclusion
Building relationships with charities requires effort and dedication. By contacting charities, understanding their work, and building relationships, you can make informed decisions about your donations and support charities that align with your values and goals.

CHAPTER 9: BEYOND DONATIONS: VOLUNTEERING AND ADVOCACY

Introduction

While donations are essential for charities, there are other ways to engage with them and make a meaningful   impact.   .

Volunteering

1. Types of Volunteering :

Explore different types of volunteering opportunities,   such   as: .

☐ Event volunteering : Helping with charity events,   fundraisers,   and   campaigns   .

☐ Skills-based volunteering : Using your skills and expertise   to   support   charities   .

☐ Project-based volunteering : Working on specific projects or initiatives with charities.   .

☐ Direct service : Working directly with people or animals in need, such as serving at a soup kitchen   or   animal   shelter.   .

☐ Behind-the-scenes : Supporting organizations through   behind-the-scenes   work,   such   as administrative   tasks   or   fundraising.   .

☐ Virtual volunteering : Volunteering remotely, such as through online tasks or virtual events.   .

2. Benefits of Volunteering :

Discuss the benefits of volunteering, including:
☐ Personal growth : Developing new skills, building confidence, and gaining experience .
☐ Making a difference : Contributing to a cause you care about and making a tangible impact .

3. Finding Volunteer Opportunities :

Provide tips on finding volunteer opportunities, such as: .
☐ Charity websites : Checking charity websites for volunteer opportunities .
☐ Volunteer platforms : Using online platforms, such as Volunteer Match or Idealist .
☐ Networking : Asking friends, family, or colleagues about volunteer opportunities.
Advocacy .

1. What is Advocacy? :

Define advocacy and its importance in creating positive change, including: .
☐ Raising awareness : Bringing attention to important issues and causes .
☐ Influencing policy : Advocating for policy changes or reforms .
☐ Empowering communities : Supporting and amplifying the voices of marginalized communities. .

2. Types of Advocacy :

Explore different types of advocacy, such as:
☐ Policy advocacy : Influencing policy decisions at local, national, or international levels
☐ Social media advocacy : Using social media to raise awareness and mobilize support

3. Benefits of Advocacy :

Discuss the benefits of advocacy, including:

 Creating systemic change : Advocating for policy changes or reforms that can have a lasting impact .

 Amplifying voices : Supporting and amplifying the voices of marginalized communities. .

 Building community : Building relationships and mobilizing community members around a shared cause. .

Getting Involved

1. Identify Your Passions :

Reflect on the causes and issues you care about and want to support. .

2. Research Charities :

Research charities and organizations working on issues you care about. .

3. Reach Out :

Contact charities or organizations directly to explore volunteer or advocacy opportunities. .

Conclusion

Volunteering and advocacy are powerful ways to engage with charities and create positive change. By donating your time, skills, or voice, you can make a meaningful impact and support causes you care about. In the next chapter, we'll explore how to evaluate the impact of your philanthropy and make adjustments as needed. .

CHAPTER 10: MEASURING SUCCESS: EVALUATING THE IMPACT OF YOUR DONATIONS

Introduction

Evaluating the impact of your donations is crucial to ensuring that your philanthropic efforts are effective and making a meaningful difference.   .

Why Measure Success ?

Measuring success is essential to effective philanthropy because it allows you to: .

1. Assess effectiveness :

Evaluate whether your donations are achieving their intended goals.   .

2. Identify areas for improvement :

Identify areas where your donations could be more effective.   .

3. Make informed decisions :

Make informed decisions about future donations based on evidence.   .

4. Maximize impact :

Maximize the impact of your donations by optimizing your giving strategy.   .

Setting Goals and Metrics

1. Define Success :

Clearly define what success means to you and your philanthropic goals.   .

2. Establish Metrics :

Establish metrics to measure the impact of your donations, such as:

▢ Output metrics : Tracking the number of people served, services provided, or goods distributed.

▢ Outcome metrics : Measuring the changes or outcomes resulting from your donations.

Approaches to Evaluation

There are several approaches to evaluating the impact of your donations, including:

1. Output-based evaluation :

Focuses on the quantity of services or products delivered.

2. Outcome-based evaluation :

Focuses on the changes or outcomes resulting from your donations.

3. Impact-based evaluation :

Focuses on the long-term, systemic changes resulting from your donations.

Key Metrics to Track

When evaluating the impact of your donations, consider tracking the following metrics:

1. Number of people served :

The number of people directly impacted by your donations.

2. Program outcomes :

The specific outcomes or changes resulting from your donations.

3. Cost-effectiveness :

The cost-effectiveness of your donations compared to other giving options.

4. Sustainability :

The sustainability of the programs or initiatives supported by your donations.

Tracking Progress
1. Regular Updates :
Request regular updates from the charity or organization, including: .
☐ Financial reports : Detailed financial reports on how your donation was used. .

2. Monitoring and Evaluation :
Monitor and evaluate the charity's performance, including: .
☐ Site visits : Visiting the charity's programs or projects to see firsthand the impact of your donation. .
☐ Meetings with staff : Meeting with charity staff to discuss progress, challenges, and future plans. .

Assessing Effectiveness
1. Evaluate Outcomes :
Evaluate the outcomes of your donations, including: .
☐ Did the charity achieve its goals? : Assess whether the charity met its objectives and made progress towards its mission. .
☐ Was the donation used effectively? : Evaluate whether the donation was used efficiently and effectively. .

2. Compare to Benchmarks :
Compare the charity's performance to benchmarks or industry standards, including: .
☐ Financial ratios : Evaluating the charity's financial health and sustainability. .
☐ Program outcomes : Comparing the charity's program outcomes to similar organizations. .

Adjusting Your Strategy
1. Refine Your Approach :

Refine your approach to philanthropy, including:
☐ Adjusting your giving strategy : Consider adjusting your giving strategy to better align with your goals and values.   .
☐ Providing feedback : Providing feedback to the charity on their performance and suggestions for improvement.   .
2. Continuously Learn :

Continuously learn and improve your philanthropic efforts, including: .
☐ Staying up-to-date on best practices : Staying current on best practices in philanthropy and evaluating their effectiveness.   .
☐ Seeking expert advice : Seeking advice from experts in philanthropy and evaluation.   .
Conclusion

Measuring the success of your donations is essential to ensuring that your philanthropic efforts are effective. By setting goals and metrics, and adjusting your strategy, you can maximize the impact of your donations and create lasting change.   .

CHAPTER 11: DONATING WITH CONFIDENCE: AVOIDING SCAMS

Introduction

As a donor, it's essential to be confident that your donations are being used effectively and efficiently. Unfortunately, scams and lack of transparency can undermine the charitable sector.

Donating with confidence is crucial because it:

1. Ensures effectiveness :

Ensures that your donations are being used to make a meaningful difference. .

2. Prevents scams :

Prevents scams and protects your financial information. .

3. Promotes transparency :

Promotes transparency and accountability in charitable giving. .

4. Builds trust :

Builds trust between donors and charitable organizations. .

Research Charities

1. Verify Legitimacy :

Research the charity's legitimacy. .

2. Check Ratings and Reviews :

Check charity ratings and reviews from: .
 Charity evaluators : Organizations like Charity Navigator. .
 Donor feedback : Reviews and testimonials from other donors. .

Avoiding Scams

1. Be Cautious of Unsolicited Requests :

Be wary of unsolicited requests for donations, especially: .
 Emails or messages : Unsolicited emails or messages asking for donations. .
 Phone calls : Unsolicited phone calls asking for donations. .

2. Watch for red flags, including:

 Lack of transparency : Charities that lack transparency about their finances, programs, or governance. .
 High-pressure tactics : Charities that use high-pressure tactics to solicit donations. .

Ensuring Transparency

1. Understand Financials :

Understand the charity's financials, including:
 Financial statements : Review the charity's financial statements. .
 Budget and expenses : Understand the charity's budget and expenses. .

2. Evaluate Governance :

Evaluate the charity's governance, including:
 Board of directors : Research the charity's board of directors and their experience. .

 Governance policies : Review the charity's governance policies and procedures.

Best Practices

1. Use Secure Donation Methods :

Use secure donation methods, such as: .
 Credit cards : Donate using a credit card, which offers protection and security.   .
 Check or wire transfer : Consider donating by check or wire transfer for larger gifts.   .

2. Get Receipts and Acknowledgments :

Get receipts and acknowledgments for your donations, including: .
 Donation receipts : Obtain a receipt for your donation, which can be used for tax purposes.
 Acknowledgment letters : Receive acknowledgment letters or emails from the charity.   .

Conclusion

Donating with confidence requires research, caution, and transparency. By following these tips, you can ensure that your donations are being used effectively and efficiently, and that you're supporting reputable charities. By being an informed and engaged donor, you can make a meaningful difference in the world.   .

CONCLUSION

We hope you've gained valuable insights and practical knowledge to inform your philanthropic journey. Donating wisely is not just about giving money; it's about making a meaningful impact, and supporting causes that matter most to you.

Empowered Donors

By reading this book, you've taken a significant step toward becoming an empowered donor. You've learned how to:

• Research and evaluate charities
• Understand financial statements and governance
• Make informed decisions about your donations
• Maximize your impact and create lasting change

Your Philanthropic Legacy

As you move forward, we encourage you to think about the kind of philanthropic legacy you want to leave. How can you make a meaningful difference in the world?

Continuing Your Journey

Philanthropy is a journey, not a destination. As you continue on your path, we recommend staying informed, engaged, and adaptable. Stay up-to-date on best practices, network with other donors and experts, and be open to new opportunities and challenges.